W9-APM-758

AMAZING AMERICA

THE 12 MOST AMAZING
AMERICAN NATURAL WONDERS

by Rebecca Rowell

12 STORY LIBRARY

www.12StoryLibrary.com

12-Story Library is an imprint of Peterson Publishing Company and Press Room Editions.

Produced for 12-Story Library by Red Line Editorial

Photographs ©: Paul B. Moore/Shutterstock Images, cover, 1; Erik Harrison/Shutterstock Images, 4, 5; kavram/Shutterstock Images, 6; Scott Prokop/Shutterstock Images, 7; Anthony Richi/Shutterstock Images, 8; Rudy Umans/Shutterstock Images, 9; Zach Frank/Shutterstock Images, 10; ColorPlayer/Thinkstock, 11; Gary Saxe/Shutterstock Images, 12; Nickolay Stanev/Shutterstock Images, 13; Henryk Sadura/Shutterstock Images, 14; Nancy Bauer/Shutterstock Images, 15; Galyna Andrushko/Shutterstock Images, 16, 28; Tom Roche/Shutterstock Images, 17; Beth Trudeau/Shutterstock Images, 18; jtbaskinphoto/Shutterstock Images, 19; Olga Bogatyrenko/Shutterstock Images, 20; ValeryRuta/Shutterstock Images, 21; Ablestock.com/Thinkstock, 22; Siim Sepp/Shutterstock Images, 23, 29; Matthew Connolly/Shutterstock Images, 24; tusharkoley/Shutterstock Images, 25; John R. McNair/Shutterstock Images, 26; SNEHIT/Shutterstock Images, 27

ISBN
978-1-63235-011-4 (hardcover)
978-1-63235-071-8 (paperback)
978-1-62143-052-0 (hosted ebook)

Library of Congress Control Number: 2014937241

Printed in the United States of America
Mankato, MN
June, 2014

Go beyond the book. Get free, up-to-date content on this topic at 12StoryLibrary.com.

TABLE OF CONTENTS

DEEP COLORS ABOUND AT GRAND CANYON

In Arizona, a huge gorge stretches 277 miles (446 km) and cuts one mile (1.6 km) into the earth. At its widest point, it measures 18 miles (29 km) across. Sunlight makes the gorge glow in hues of red, orange, brown, gray, green, pink, and violet. This unique place is the Grand Canyon.

Its massive size and range of colors attract millions of people each year. The colors are from layers of rocks such as granite, limestone,

The Grand Canyon became a national park in 1919.

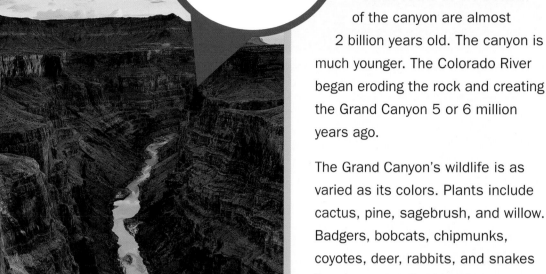

The Colorado River flows through the Grand Canyon.

sandstone, and schist. Some rocks at the bottom of the canyon are almost 2 billion years old. The canyon is much younger. The Colorado River began eroding the rock and creating the Grand Canyon 5 or 6 million years ago.

The Grand Canyon's wildlife is as varied as its colors. Plants include cactus, pine, sagebrush, and willow. Badgers, bobcats, chipmunks, coyotes, deer, rabbits, and snakes live there, too. Bald eagles glide through the skies over the canyon. And trout swim in its waters.

VIEW FROM ABOVE

In 2007, Skywalk opened at the Grand Canyon. This horseshoe-shaped balcony juts out approximately 70 feet (20 m) from the canyon's edge and 4,000 feet (1,200 m) above the ground. It is enclosed, with a metal frame and glass sides. The clear floor allows those brave enough to look straight down to the canyon floor far below.

21

Number of miles (34 km) people hike from the North Rim to the South Rim.

Location: Northern Arizona
Park: Grand Canyon National Park
Annual visitors: 5 million

LIFE THRIVES IN DEATH VALLEY

Death Valley is the hottest place on Earth and the driest in North America. Summer temperatures regularly top 120 degrees Fahrenheit (49°C) in the shade. Rocks and sand soak up the sunlight, and the heat is trapped between the high walls of the valley. But the weather is much more pleasant from late autumn to spring. That's when visitors flock to Death Valley to see the surrounding landscape of desert, canyons, mountains, and sand dunes.

Death Valley is in southeastern California. It is approximately 140 miles (225 km) long and 5 to 15 miles (8 to 24 km) wide. Its lowest spot, Badwater Basin, is 282 feet (86 m) below sea level. That measurement makes Death Valley the lowest place in North America.

The hot, dry climate makes water evaporate quickly. The region doesn't have much water to begin with. Less than two inches (5 cm) of rain usually falls each year. Though its name suggests

At Death Valley's Zabriskie Point, erosion has sculpted the land into sharp ridges.

Death Valley is the largest national park in the continental United States.

134

World record highest temperature in degrees Fahrenheit (57°C), recorded in Death Valley in 1913.

Location: California
Park: Death Valley National Park
Annual visitors: Approximately 800,000

otherwise, many living things thrive in the valley. Some plants survive because their deep roots can reach water underground. Many desert animals come out only at night. Others spend part of the year up in the mountains, where it is cooler. Kangaroo rats, rabbits, squirrels, lizards, scorpions, and snakes all live in Death Valley.

EVERGLADES OVERFLOWS WITH EXOTIC WILDLIFE

Only one place in the world is home to both alligators and crocodiles. It's the Everglades, the only subtropical wilderness in the United States. The Everglades is teeming with exotic wildlife. It has 27 types of snakes and more than 350 species of birds. Several endangered animals live in the Everglades, too, including the American crocodile, the Florida panther, the manatee, and several types of sea turtle.

The Everglades covers 4,300 square miles (11,100 sq km) of southern Florida with marshland. Each year, the Everglades gets approximately 50 inches (130 cm) of rain. The rain

The Everglades is actually a very slow-moving river.

80

Number of Florida panthers that live in the Everglades. This is the Everglades' most endangered animal.

Location: Southern Florida
Park: Everglades National Park -
Annual visitors: More than 1 million

INVASIVE SPECIES

Nonnative plants and animals have been introduced in the Everglades. They can cause problems for the native species. The water hyacinth blocks sunlight needed by the wildlife growing below it. And the Nile monitor, a type of lizard, eats crocodile eggs and burrowing owls. The Brazilian peppertree, Burmese python, and Cuban tree frog are other nonnative examples.

causes Lake Okeechobee in the northern Everglades to overflow. The water moves slowly southward in a shallow river that is filled with wild grasses. It flows through cypress swamps, wet prairie, and groves of small trees and shrubs. Then it drains into Florida Bay. The dry season spans from December to April. It is easiest to view wildlife during this time, as animals are drawn to the remaining water sources.

The American alligator is the biggest of approximately 50 reptile species that live in the Everglades.

MASSIVE MAMMOTH CAVE LIES UNDER KENTUCKY

Imagine a maze more than 400 miles (644 km) long. Next, imagine it is underground. Such a place exists at Mammoth Cave. Located in Kentucky, Mammoth is the longest known cave system in the world. It is so big that the second- and third-longest caves would both fit inside with 100 miles (161 km) to spare.

Stalactites and stalagmites form as dripping water leaves behind deposits of a mineral called calcium carbonate.

10

Miles (16 km) of cave open to tourists.

Location: Kentucky
Park: Mammoth Cave National Park
Annual visitors: 390,000

THINK ABOUT IT

Many of the rock formations in Mammoth Cave are fragile. What do you think visitors could do to help keep them safe?

Mammoth is not a single cave, though. It is a system of caves that developed in limestone as water wore the rock away. Some of the water is still there, in underground rivers and lakes. Spiky rock formations called stalactites hang from the ceilings and walls. Similar stalagmites rise up from the ground.

These were formed as dripping water slowly deposited minerals. Some of these formations have names, such as Frozen Niagara and Pillars of Hercules.

Mammoth also has wildlife. Inhabitants include types of crayfish and fish that do not have eyes. They do not need them in the darkness of the cave.

The temperature inside the caves stays around 54 degrees Fahrenheit (12°C) year-round.

BIG TREES TOWER IN GIANT FOREST

In central California, some trees grow as high as a 26-story building. Their diameters at the ground are greater than the width of many streets. This special type of tree has several different names. One is simply "big tree." It is also known as the Sierra redwood and the giant sequoia. More than 8,000 of these biggest trees on the planet are in the Giant Forest. The forest is in the Sierra Nevada mountain range.

The Giant Forest's massive sequoias are quite old. Scientists estimate the trees are between 1,800 and 2,700 years old. They can find out the age by counting the rings on a tree stump. Most of the largest

The big trees of the Giant Forest dwarf visitors.

JOHN MUIR

The Giant Forest is here today because of the dedication of John Muir (1838–1914). This Scottish-American author loved nature and spent considerable time exploring the wilderness, especially the Sierra Nevada mountain range. He helped create several national parks, including Sequoia and Yosemite. In 1901, Muir published *Our National Parks.* He wanted his book to help readers to understand and see the beauty of the parks he enjoyed.

trees have names. General Sherman in National Sequoia Park is the biggest of them all. It measures 102.6 feet (31.3 m) around its base, and 274.9 feet (83.8 m) high. These trees never stop growing. They usually die only if they are cut down or destroyed by extreme weather.

52,500

Cubic feet (1,500 m³) of wood in General Sherman, the world's largest tree.

Location: California
Park: Sequoia and Kings Canyon National Parks
Annual visitors: 1.5 million to both parks

General Sherman has the largest volume of any tree in the world.

MISSISSIPPI CARVES SCENIC PATH THROUGH AMERICA

A river begins in Lake Itasca in northern Minnesota. It travels approximately 2,340 miles (3,770 km) south until it reaches New Orleans, Louisiana. Along the way, it touches 10 states. Algonquin-speaking peoples called it *misi sipi*, which means "Father of Waters."

The Mississippi is the longest river in North America. At Lake Itasca, it is at its narrowest, measuring 20 to 30 feet (6 to 9 m) across. It reaches its widest point at Lake Winnibigoshish in Minnesota. There, the river spans more than 11 miles (18 km). The Upper Mississippi

The Mississippi River has more than 260 species of fish.

The Mississippi River borders 10 states. Here, it makes up part of the border between Wisconsin and Iowa.

winds its way through prairie land and forests and cuts between limestone bluffs. It joins with the St. Croix and Minnesota rivers in the Twin Cities.

3

Miles per hour (5 km/h) the river moves at its mouth in New Orleans, Louisiana.

Location: Minnesota south to Louisiana

Park: Mississippi National River and Recreation Area in St. Paul, Minnesota

Locks and dams: 29 on the Upper Mississippi

Near St. Louis, Missouri, it joins with the Missouri River. As the rivers meet, the current picks up and the water becomes muddier. Near Cairo, Illinois, the Mississippi meets up with the mighty Ohio River. The river swells to more than twice the size it is north of that point. Finally, it dumps into the Gulf of Mexico.

The Mississippi's watershed is larger than 1 million square miles (2.6 million sq km). That means all the waterways in that area drain into the Mississippi. The watershed area includes land in 31 states. The river provides water to more than 50 cities.

MOUNT McKINLEY REACHES GREAT HEIGHTS IN ALASKA

At 20,320 feet (6,194 m), this peak rises higher than any other point in North America. The Athabaskan Indians called it *Denali*, which means "the high one" or "the great one."

Russians call it *Bolshaya Gora*, or "Great Mountain." Its common name is Mount McKinley.

Mount McKinley is located in Alaska. It stands near the middle of the Alaska Range. The mountain's

Mount McKinley is the third-tallest mountain in the world.

top half is covered with snow and glaciers. Some of the glaciers are more than 30 miles (48 km) long. Temperatures can drop as low as minus 75 degrees Fahrenheit (−59°C). Windchills can be as cold as minus 118 degrees Fahrenheit (−83°C). Such temperatures can be deadly quickly. The harsh climate doesn't stop people from climbing McKinley. As many as 32,000 people have tried to reach its peak.

11

Age of Jordan Romero, the youngest person to reach Mount McKinley's summit.

Location: Alaska
Park: Denali National Park and Preserve
Annual visitors: 400,000

About half of them succeeded at reaching the top.

Mount McKinley was named after President William McKinley.

OLD FAITHFUL ERUPTS ALMOST LIKE CLOCKWORK

Hikers cluster together at viewing spots and wait in suspense. For a while, nothing happens. Then suddenly, a burst of hot water and steam shoots up from the ground. It continues for another few minutes before dying down. But it will happen again in an hour or two.

Old Faithful isn't the biggest or highest geyser in Yellowstone National Park. But it is the most

YELLOWSTONE

The world has many thousands of hydrothermal sites. Approximately 10,000 of them are in Yellowstone National Park, including Old Faithful. The park occupies land in Wyoming, Montana, and Idaho. Yellowstone became the first national park in the United States and the world on March 1, 1872.

Old Faithful is Yellowstone's most popular geyser because it erupts so frequently.

regular. It got its name because it erupts faithfully, or regularly. Every 60 to 110 minutes, Old Faithful sends water 130 to 140 feet (40 to 43 m) into the air. Sometimes, the spout reaches higher than 180 feet (55 m). Eruptions last from 90 seconds to more than five minutes. During that time, the geyser spits out 3,700 to 8,400 gallons (14,000 to 32,000 L) of boiling water.

Old Faithful is the most famous of Yellowstone's more than 300 geysers. Volcanoes and earthquakes have been active in the area for millions of years. Geysers are the result of hot volcanic rocks heating groundwater. When the water boils, it bursts through the surface.

Old Faithful's highest recorded eruption reached 185 feet (56 m) into the air.

203
Approximate temperature in degrees Fahrenheit (95°C) of the water that erupts from Old Faithful.

Location: Wyoming
Park: Yellowstone National Park
Annual visitors: 3 million

THINK ABOUT IT

Why is creating national parks important? What might happen if the government did not create and care for places such as Yellowstone?

THREE WATERFALLS MAKE UP SPECTACULAR NIAGARA

Rushing water crashes down at a rate of 750,000 gallons (2.8 million L) per second. That is the most of any waterfall in the United States. Visitors wear ponchos to experience the falls from up close. They climb wooden staircases through the stormy mist to an observation deck. Or they can ride boats through the churning waters at the waterfall's base.

Water flow over the falls is greatest in June, July, and August.

20

Approximate percentage of the world's freshwater that goes over Niagara Falls.

Location: New York State and Ontario, Canada

Park: Niagara Falls State Park, Niagara Falls National Heritage Site

Annual visitors: 22.5 million

Niagara Falls is on the border between New York and Ontario, Canada. Niagara is actually three waterfalls. Two islands separate them: Luna and Goat. American Falls and Bridal Veil Falls are on the American side of Niagara Falls. American Falls is approximately 830 feet (253 m) wide and 180 feet (55 m) high. Bridal Veil is much smaller. It is approximately 56 feet (17 m) wide and 78 feet (24 m) high. Horseshoe Falls, on the Canadian side, is the biggest. It is approximately 2,200 feet (670 m) wide and 185 feet (56 m) high.

Water from four Great Lakes—Superior, Michigan, Huron, and Erie—makes its way into the Niagara River. After the water drops over the falls, it ends up in Lake Ontario.

The Niagara River is deepest just below the falls.

KILAUEA VOLCANO'S ERUPTIONS CARVE RUGGED LANDSCAPE

Rugged, dark, and barren may not be the first words to come to mind when people think of Hawaii, but they fit. The fiftieth state is home to a geologic feature with a harsh, rocky landscape. It is Kilauea, the world's most active volcano.

Located on the Big Island of Hawaii, Kilauea reaches 4,090 feet (1,250 m) into the air. The volcano's name is Hawaiian for "much spreading." Kilauea is a wide dome formed by lava that erupted from within the earth. The lava has created a tough landscape very different from the moist, green,

Kilauea has had more than 60 eruptions since 1983.

500

Approximate number of acres (200 ha) of new land Kilauea has added to the island of Hawaii since 1983.

Location: Hawaii Big Island

Park: Hawaii Volcanoes National Park

Annual visitors: 2.6 million

THINK ABOUT IT

Think about living near a volcano such as Kilauea. What would be the benefits and drawbacks? Would it be worth living there?

colorful environment typical of the Pacific paradise.

Kilauea sits in a crater that formed when its cone collapsed. The crater is almost three miles (5 km) long and two miles (3 km) wide. And it is 500 feet (150 m) deep.

People love visiting Kilauea. But the volcano has also sent people fleeing. From 1983 to 1999, Kilauea's lava threatened nearby neighborhoods. The molten rock buried eight miles (13 km) of highway and destroyed 181 houses and a visitor center.

Kilauea is the world's most active volcano.

VOLCANO EXPLODED TO FORM CRATER LAKE

Almost 7,000 years ago, Mount Mazama reached as high as 12,000 feet (3,700 m) into the sky. The volcano was part of the Cascade Mountains in modern-day Oregon. When Mazama erupted, its top blew apart. Over time, a new feature developed in the crater Mazama left behind: a lake.

Crater Lake is 1,943 feet (592 m) deep. It is the deepest lake in the

THE ISLAND AND THE OLD MAN

Wizard Island sits in Crater Lake. Like the lake, the island was created by volcanic activity. The island is a cone that formed from volcanic debris.

A log has been floating on end in Crater Lake for more than a century. People named it "Old Man." Winds blow it to different spots in the lake.

Crater Lake is known as one of the clearest lakes in the world.

This small island in Crater Lake is called Phantom Ship.

7

Crater Lake's world ranking for depth—it's the seventh-deepest lake on the planet.

Location: Oregon
Park: Crater Lake National Park
Annual visitors: 500,000

United States. The lake is known for its rich blue color. The brilliant hue results from a lack of sediment, which would come from a river. But the water in Crater Lake does not come from a river. It is formed by precipitation. Crater Lake gets more than 44 feet (13 m) of snow each year. It's so much snow that not all of it melts until the beginning of August. As it melts, it flows into the lake.

ROCKY MOUNTAINS RISE ACROSS WESTERN UNITED STATES

A jagged line of sharp peaks stretches for approximately 3,000 miles (4,800 km). In some places, the mountain range is more than 300 miles (480 km) wide. The Rocky Mountains, or Rockies, dominate the western United States. The range even reaches into Canada.

VALUABLE MOUNTAINS

The Rocky Mountains offer more than beautiful scenery and slopes for skiing. The Rockies also hold valuable materials. People have mined copper, gold, silver, and other metals. Miners have found sapphires, too. Oil and natural gas also are found there.

Pike's Peak in the Rocky Mountains is the second most visited mountain peak in the world.

14,433

Height in feet (4,399 m) of Colorado's Mount Elbert, the highest peak of the Rockies.

Location: Western North America, stretching from Alberta and British Columbia, Canada, to New Mexico

Park: Rocky Mountain National Park

Annual visitors: More than 3,000,000

At least 100 mountain ranges make up the chain. Many of the Rockies' summits reach higher than 13,000 feet (4,000 m). The giant range includes valleys, rivers, and glaciers, too.

Plants and animals thrive in the Rockies. The wildlife varies from north to south. Being high or low on the mountain makes a difference, too. Pine trees thrive in the middle elevations. Colorful flowers dot high meadows. Black bears and grizzly bears live in the Rockies with mountain lions and wolverines. And bighorn sheep and deer move up and down the mountains during different seasons.

The gently sloping Mount Elbert is the highest point in the Rockies. Its top is reachable by bicycle.

FACT SHEET

- Many of the United States' natural wonders are now part of national parks. On March 1, 1872, President Ulysses S. Grant signed a law creating the first national park: Yellowstone. In 1916, President Woodrow Wilson signed a law creating the National Park Service. The goal of the law was to keep and care for natural wonders and wildlife for people to enjoy, including future generations. Today, the national park system has 401 sites. In addition to national parks, the system includes battlefields and other historic places, lakes and seashores, monuments, recreation areas, rivers, and trails.

- People have lived in the Grand Canyon for thousands of years. Artifacts have shown inhabitants were there almost 12,000 years ago. Today, several Native American tribes call the canyon home. They include the Hualapai, the Havasupai, the Hopi, the Navajo, the Paiute, and the Zuni.

- Death Valley's high temperatures and dry landscape do not keep tourists away. Hundreds of thousands of people visit each year. Some bike and hike there. Some watch birds. And some camp.

- Several organizations work to preserve the country's natural wonders and wildlife. The National Audubon Society strives to maintain and restore ecosystems, such as the Everglades. The organization focuses on birds in particular. John Muir founded the Sierra Club in 1892 to protect the environment.

- Before it became a protected landmark, Mammoth Cave was used for other purposes. During the War of 1812, people mined minerals to make gunpowder. Later, people used it as a hospital for patients with tuberculosis, a disease that usually affects the lungs.

- Technology lets people enjoy some natural wonders from home. Yellowstone National Park has a webcam focused on Old Faithful. People can watch the geyser erupt online as it happens. Niagara Falls can be viewed online, too.

- Natural wonders are not only pretty places. People rely on the Mississippi River for water, transportation, and recreation. Residents near Niagara rely on it for electricity. A power plant there uses Niagara's natural power to create electricity. Niagara Falls produces the most power of any power plant in New York.

- Glaciers are also natural wonders. These giant sheets of ice cover more than 30,000 square miles (78,000 sq km) of the United States. Most of the country's glaciers are in Alaska. The largest is Bering Glacier. It is 127 miles (204 km) long.

GLOSSARY

elevation
How high a place is.

evaporate
To change from a liquid to a gas.

freshwater
Water that is not salty.

geyser
A spring that shoots hot water and steam through the earth's surface.

hydrothermal
Water heated by melted rock under the earth's surface.

inhabit
To live in or occupy a place.

lava
Melted rock that comes out of a volcano.

precipitation
Water that falls to the ground as rain or snow.

sea level
The level of the surface of the sea.

sediment
Materials such as stone and sand that are carried in water.

stalactite
A pointed piece of rock hanging down from the ceiling of a cave, formed by dripping water depositing minerals.

stalagmite
A pointed piece of rock that sticks up from the floor of a cave, formed by dripping water depositing minerals.

subtropical
Regions near the tropical zone.

watershed
The area that drains into a river.

FOR MORE INFORMATION

Books

DeFries, Cheryl. *What Are the Seven Natural Wonders of the United States?* Berkeley Heights, NJ: Enslow, 2013.

Frisch, Nate. *Grand Canyon National Park*. Mankato, MN: Creative Paperbacks, 2014.

McHugh, Erin. *National Parks: A Kid's Guide to America's Parks, Monuments, and Landmarks*. New York: Black Dog & Leventhal, 2012.

National Geographic Kids National Parks Guide USA. Washington, DC: National Geographic Society, 2012.

Woods, Michael, and Mary B. Woods. *Seven Natural Wonders of North America*. Minneapolis, MN: Twenty-First Century Books, 2009.

Websites

Kids Discover Spotlight: National Parks
www.kidsdiscover.com/spotlight/national-parks-for-kids

National Park Service
www.nps.gov/index.htm

Natural Wonders of North America
naturalwondersofnorthamerica.com

INDEX

About the Author

Rebecca Rowell has authored books for young readers on a variety of topics. She has a master's degree in publishing and writing from Emerson College and lives in Minneapolis, Minnesota.